Hi there,

My name is Toby, and I am a Dalmatian.

After the huge success of my first book of dog walks (thank you if you bought one), I was inundated with ideas for new walks from all my canine friends. There were so many that I have decided to bring out a second book of walks in South Devon. It is amazing how many beautiful places there are for dogs and their owners to have a nice stroll.

If this is the first time you have seen one of my books then you might want to buy Book 1 as well.

As I love to play, I will try and let you know if you are likely to meet any other dogs to play with or to sniff.
I will try and let you know about all the good things and any not so good features of any walk.

I will also let you know if there are any poo bins for your walker, as they don't seem to like poo as much as we do.

Enjoy your new walks,

Toby

Email me:
toby@scrivenhousebooks.co.uk

Walk 1 - Chercombe Valley

Grid Reference: 823 720—Landranger 202   Distance: 4 miles (2 hours)

This is a lovely walk along the River Lemon with quite a few fields, but we hardly ever met any cows in all the time we have done it. I think a lot of the farmland is just used for crops.

1. Take the Ashburton Road (A383) out of Newton Abbot and pull into the layby oppos the entrance to Seale Hayne college. Get your walkers to put you on the lead and then walk about 100 yards down the wide grass verge (away from Newton Abbot, towards the converted barns) until you get to a footpath sign on your left just before the barns.
2. Follow the footpath sign down a short lane towards a field. Go into the field and foll the track down to the bottom corner where you cross a small footbridge into the nex field, I love to have a quick splash here.
3. Follow the River Lemon along the edge of the field until you reach the bottom of a small dam. My walker says it's something to do with flood protection.
4. Follow the path up the side of the dam and down the other side.
5. At the bottom of the slope you will see an obvious woodland footpath on your left which is signposted. Follow this track along the edge of the woods.
6. Get your walker to put you on your lead at the end of the track as it opens out onto quiet country lane. Turn right down the lane for a short distance.
7. The footpath then turns into a field on the left, opposite a renovated cottage. Follow the footpath across the next three fields, following the River Lemon.
8. At the end of the third field you come out onto a road that can be busy, so get back the lead. Cross the road and continue on the path off left, next to the house, and c tinue following the river. Now there are lots of opportunities for sticks and paddles.
9. The path now follows the River Lemon all the way along the left bank to Baker's P in Newton Abbot. You can cross the River Lemon in Baker's Park and come back the other side until you reach a familiar bridge to cross back to join the original wa

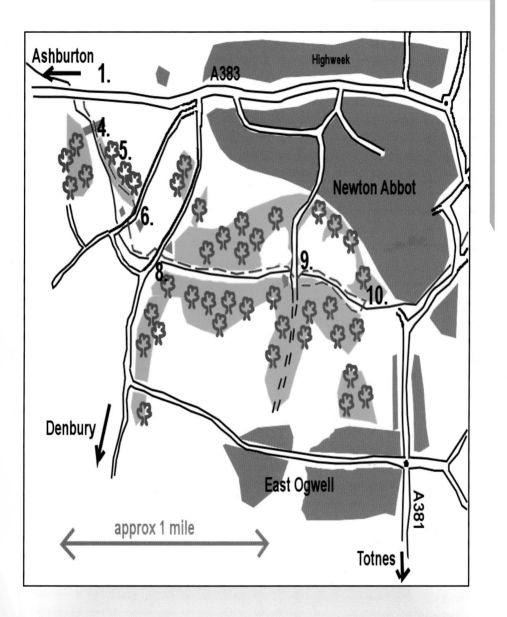

Playmates?	Y	Water to play in?	Y	Running space?	Y
Are there any hills?	Y	Any tricky stiles?	N	Car Parking?	Y
Are farm animals likely?	Y	Poo Bins?	Y	Plenty of sticks?	Y

Walk 2 - Long Woods - Kingswear

Grid Reference: 885 528—Landranger 202   Distance: 2miles (1 hour)

This is another lovely walk above the banks of the River Dart. You could do it just on its own or add it to the Hoodown walk from Book 1. The views of the Dart are absolutely beautiful and well worth the walk. Great blackberries in late August.

1. Get your walker to head for Kingswear in the car and take the road towards the Higher Ferry (A379). As you get to the bottom of the hill you will see a big sign on your right for Noss Marina, there is also a sign for the Long Woods walk and car park. Turn right here and park up in the car park.
2. The entrance to the walk is opposite the car park.
3. Once you have started the walk you will notice a sign warning about adders. On a sunny day you may want to stay on the lead for the first five minutes of the walk. I have not seen any adders on my walks here, but my walker says that, 'you never know'.
4. The rest of the walk is easy just follow the Dart Valley Trail signs until you get some spectacular views of the river. Then keep going until you have had enough. Then turn round and head back to the car park.
5. If you are feeling really adventurous you can follow the trail all the way to Greenway and get the passenger ferry across to the pub in Dittisham before turning back.

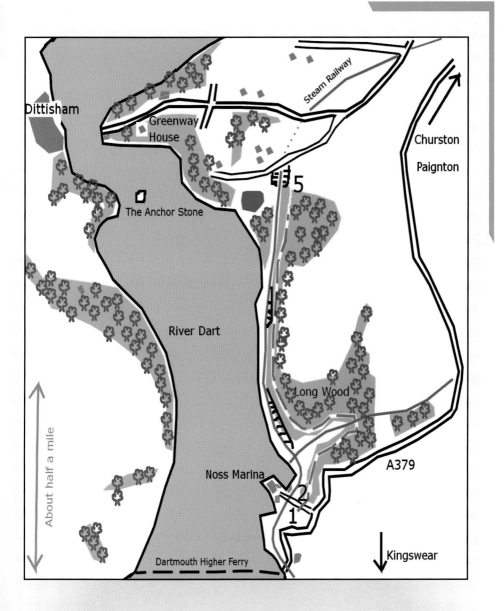

Playmates?	Y	Water to play in?	N	Running space?	Y
Are there any hills?	Y	Any tricky stiles?	N	Car Parking?	Y
Are farm animals likely?	N	Poo Bins?	N	Plenty of sticks?	Y

Walk 3 - Stowford Mill - Ivybridge

Grid Reference: 635 570—-Landranger 202   Distance: 3 miles (1.5 hours)

This is a fantastic walk on the edge of the moors. Another great viaduct, loads of water and lots of friends to play with. If it has been raining you really need wellies if you opt to walk back along the King's Gutter.

1. Take the A38 to Ivybridge and turn into the town up Western Road. When you get to the bottom end of the high street you have to bare right up Marjorie Kelly Way because the high street is one way. Follow the road and then take a left at the roundabout up Leonards Road. Then at the next junction turn left again, along Fore Street
2. Cross the river and then turn right up Erme Road and drive straight on into Station Road, then drive along until you see the viaduct. There is a small car park on the right with a poo bin. Get your owner to park here.
3. Now head off under the viaduct and follow the path along the river's edge.
4. After about a mile you reach the end of the path. If your walker looks tired they may want to go back the way they came. Otherwise take a left turn up some 'steps' that lead up into the woods.
5. The path then bends left back down the river and soon turns into a recognisable walled channel, the King's Gutter. Follow this all the way along until you come to a normally quiet road. Follow the road downhill for about 5 metres until you see a pat leading downhill back into the woods on your left.
6. {Note: before you take this path you could opt to cross straight over the road and through another small gate, following the King's Gutter a little further. After about 5 minutes the path will turn sharply right up a moorland hill. Walk a few paces up the hill and enjoy the views, then return the way you came and rejoin the walk}

7. Follow this path down into the woods, back to the river again. At the river, turn right and follow the path back to the car park.

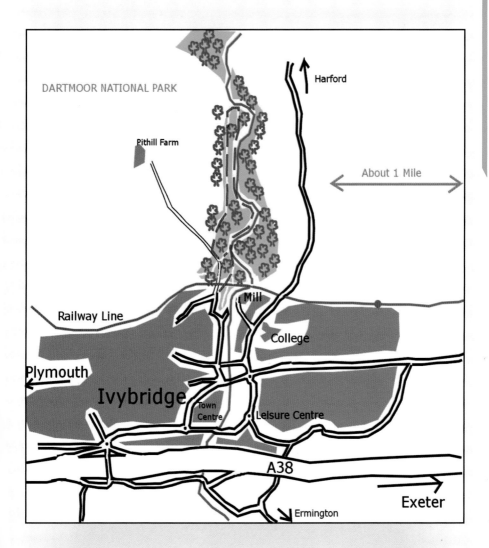

Playmates?	Y	Water to play in?	Y	Running space?	Y
Are there any hills?	Y	Any tricky stiles?	N	Car Parking?	Y
Are farm animals likely?	N	Poo Bins?	Y	Plenty of sticks?	Y

Walk 4 - Wall's Hill - Torquay

| Grid Reference: 928 653 Landranger 202 | Distance: 1.5 miles (1 hour) |

I can almost guarantee that you'll meet other doggy friends to play with on this walk. Lots of space to run around and fantastic views for your walkers.

1. From Torquay Harbour take Torwood Street until it becomes Babbacombe Road. As you reach Babbacombe there is a turn on the right with a small signpost saying Babbacombe Downs, opposite The Rose pub. Take this right turn, then immediately turn right again into Wall's Hill Road, also signposted for Babbacombe Cricket Club.
2. My walkers normally park in the pay and display car park as it is only £1 and makes the walk a little longer. Make sure you get on the lead whilst you cross the car park.
3. Walk up onto the obvious common and then go straight across the cricket field (avoiding the fenced off pitch). Please ask your walkers to put you on a lead and take you around the edge if lots of humans in white are playing fetch with a big stick and a ball. They get annoyed when doggies join in.
4. Now go up the small hill on the other side of the cricket pitch and walk straight on to the far corner of the common, towards the sea. Enjoy the views right across to Exmouth, and Portland Bill (on a clear day).
5. Follow the track through the hedge and then follow the perimeter fence around the second common enjoying more lovely views and lots of sniffs. You will see a cove below, this is Anstey's Cove, famous for smugglers!
6. On the other side of the common you will find a Coast Path signpost. If your walkers are still waggy tailed and fancy some real exercise you can take this path down to the cove (Warning: there are a couple of bits of the path that are a bit steep, which some walkers may find tricky). If you don't fancy the cove. Enjoy the common before going home.
7. If you follow the path to the cove, you will come to a left turn signposted 'Coast Path' Take this and follow the steps down to the road.
8. Get your walkers to put you on the lead for about 50 metres until you join the steps and tarmac track on the left that lead down to the cove. In the summer you can get an ice-cream at the bottom.
9. After you have searched for smugglers Go back the way you came. Slowly!

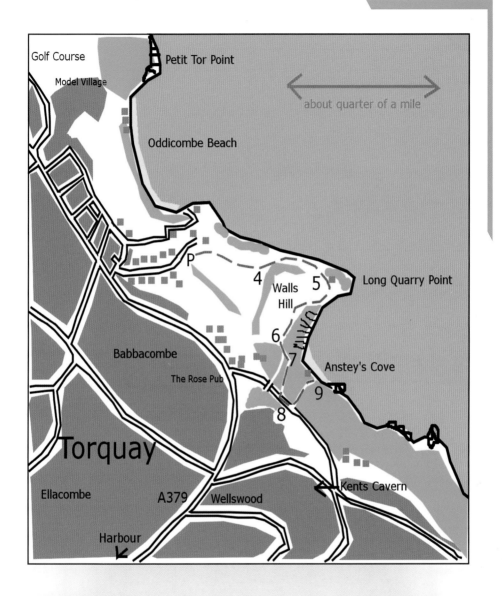

Playmates?	Y	Water to play in?	Y	Running space?	Y
Are there any hills?	Y	Any tricky stiles?	N	Car Parking?	Y
Are farm animals likely?	N	Poo Bins?	Y	Plenty of sticks?	Y

Walk 5— Little Haldon-Teignmouth

Grid Reference: 918 764 Landranger 192   Distance: 1 mile (40 mins)

This is a lovely short walk, with amazing views across to Dartmoor. We love doing this walk early in the morning or in the evening as the sun sets over the moor.

1. There are two ways to find this walk. From Exeter you can take the first Teignmouth turning off the A380 and follow signs for the B3192. From Torquay you need to head towards Exeter and take the same junction (it is past the Ugborough and Ideford turn). You will drive through Pine woods for a short while then past fields. There will be a sign on your left to Ashcombe. You will then go uphill with woods on your left, up onto Little Haldon Common. You go straight on at a junction signposted to Dawlish on your left, you then pass a car park on your left with large boulders at the entrance. Take the next right. You should now have a golf course on your left. At the next crossroads go straight ahead and park in the car park immediately on your right.
2. Once you have parked you need to get your lead on and take your walkers back to the car park entrance.
3. From here turn left and walk back down the road, crossing straight across the crossroads.
4. On the other side of the crossroads you will see a narrow path leading off on your left. Follow this onto the common and then follow the path straight ahead.
5. At the fork take a left and follow the path on its circular route, which will eventually return you to the same fork and back to the road.

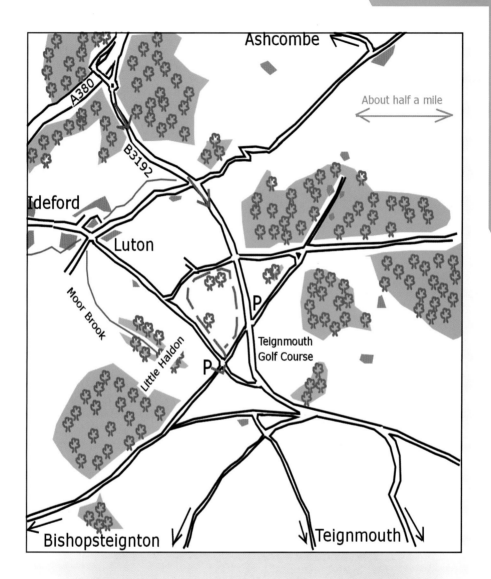

Playmates?	Y	Water to play in?	N	Running space?	Y
Are there any hills?	N	Any tricky stiles?	N	Car Parking?	Y
Are farm animals likely?	N	Poo Bins?	N	Plenty of sticks?	N

Walk 6 - Clennon Valley - Paignton

Grid Reference: 889 595—Landranger 202   Distance: 1 mile (30 minutes)

A short walk in Paignton, but with the lovely little lakes it is well worth a stroll. My brother Domino often goes on this walk while Izzy and Maisy have a swim in the nearby leisure centre. As you know Dalmatians aren't that keen on the water, especially with chlorine in it!

1. Park at Goodrington Leisure Centre in Paignton. Your walkers will need a bit of change for the pay and display.
2. Send any swimmers off to the pool.
3. Walk to the bottom of the car park as if you are heading around the back of the Leisure Centre. If you turn right, along the back of the building you will find a gate that opens out onto Clennon Valley Playing Fields. Follow the path up through the playing fields.
4. Take the left turn on the path down the side of one football pitch.
5. Then head for the path that leads behind the lakes.
6. Follow the path behind the lakes. You could even stop and feed the ducks, I prefer to just stare at them menacingly.
7. The path then leads you back around the top of the playing fields, you then make you way back down past the football pitches, back to the leisure centre.

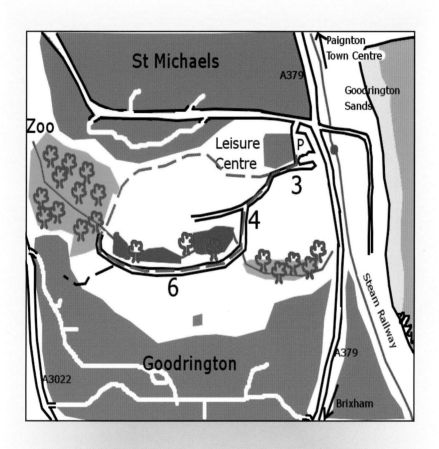

Playmates?	Y	Water to play in?	N	Running space?	Y
Are there any hills?	N	Any tricky stiles?	N	Car Parking?	Y
Are farm animals likely?	N	Poo Bins?	Y	Plenty of sticks?	Y

Walk 7 - Saltram House - Plymouth

Grid Reference— 525 559 Landranger 201   Distance: 2.5 miles (1.5 hrs)

This is a great walk, especially out of the main tourist season, as you can allow your dog off the lead if it is well behaved. Great views, and at least eight poo bins!!

1. From the A38 Marsh Mills roundabout outside Plymouth, head towards Plympton, then follow brown tourist signs towards Saltram House.
2. As you enter the grounds of Saltram House there is a rough car park in the woods to your right, almost immediately after you go through the first gates off the main road. This is the dog walker's car park, so park here. Please get your walkers to put you o your lead. If there are lots of visitors around the National Trust would ask you to stay on the lead. We go in the evenings or off season when there a very few people apar from other dog walkers around, so this is not a problem. The gates are open all yea round from dawn to dusk.
3. You then walk through the woods following the road on into Saltram. You will cross the A38 on a large bridge with great views of traffic (if you like that sort of thing).
4. Immediately after the bridge you have to turn left along a gravel track that runs alon the top of some fields.
5. About 100 metres on you will find a path that leads down between the fields toward the main house. Take this path down the hill.
6. When you get to the bottom you need to head diagonally right following a tarmac road downhill. This is signposted to the Estate Office. The road then forks, left to th Estate office and right down a hill to the Riverside Walk.
7. Take the right hand path and follow the tarmac track down the hill. At the bottom yc will walk around the side of some gates across the track. The Riverside walk then curves off to the left following the outside of the woods. Follow this gravel track around to the left and then follow it all the way along the river bank. Do not follow tl tarmac track.

8 After a lovely long walk along the riverside the path bends up towards the main house. At the top of this small hill, a path will lead off to the left. Ignore this path and carry straight on.

9 A bit further on the path takes a sharp left and turns into a tarmac road again. Follow this road all the way back to the main house. Then take the track back up between the two fields, back across the A38 bridge and back to your car.

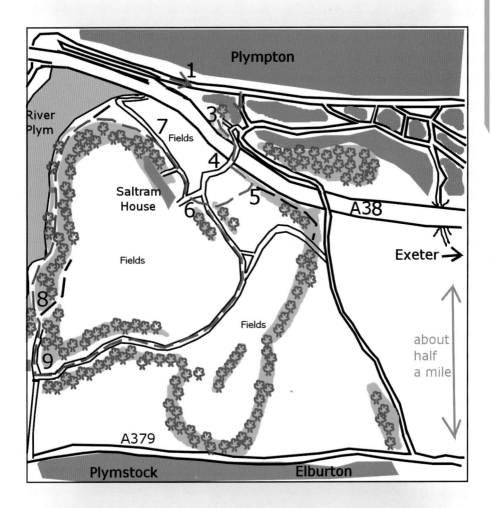

Playmates?	Y	Water to play in?	N	Running space?	Y
Are there any hills?	Y	Any tricky stiles?	N	Car Parking?	Y
Are farm animals likely?	N	Poo Bins?	Y	Plenty of sticks?	Y

Walk 8 - Gara Bridge - South Hams

Grid Reference: 725 547—Landranger 202   Distance: 3.5 mile (2 hours)

This is a lovely walk tucked away in the South Hams. You will need to wear wellies for this walk, if it has been raining. Lovely river, with some nice places for a picnic on the way back up.

1. From the A38 (travelling towards Plymouth) take the exit after South Brent, sign-posted for Ermington and Ugborough. As the road takes a sharp right go straight on and follow this lane until you get to California Cross turn left towards Gara Bridge and Moreleigh. Follow the lane for a short distance then take the next left (near a caravan park) and follow the lane. Eventually the lane heads quite steeply downhill and bares sharp left. There is room for one car to park on the right next to a clearly signposted footpath. Beware there is another footpath sign before this one, in a field entrance.
2. Once you have parked, follow the path down to the River Avon and along the bank. This bit can be a bit muddy when it has rained. There were lovely daffodils here when we visited. Now simply follow the path all the way along the river bank.
3. Eventually you arrive at Gara Bridge. Get your walker to put you on the lead here, as the road can be quite busy. You now need to cross the road and walk facing the oncoming traffic. Walk down to the bridge and into the hamlet.
4. Turn left and follow the bridlepath back up the opposite side of the river.
5. After about 0.5 of a mile you will descend to an open area by the river which can be nice for a picnic. I love to paddle here and have a drink.
6. Once you have had enough, carry on up the path, do not follow the old railway line as it is a dead end.
7. You will see a few signposts, carry straight on. The track eventually turns into a road, and passes through a friendly farmyard. The dog here barks but he also wagged his tail and was fine with me.
8. Follow the quiet lane up to the next hamlet at Bickham Bridge. At the T-junction turn left.
9. Then follow this lane until at the next t-junction you take another left. Then follow the river Avon back to the car.

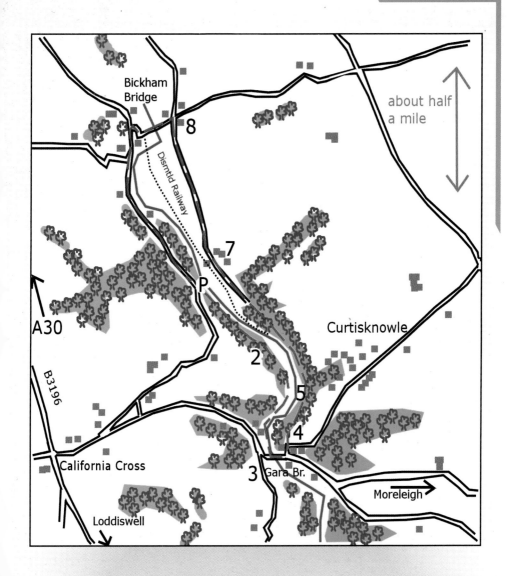

Playmates?	Y	Water to play in?	Y	Running space?	Y
Are there any hills?	Y	Any tricky stiles?	N	Car Parking?	N
Are farm animals likely?	N	Poo Bins?	N	Plenty of sticks?	Y

Walk 9 - Occombe Valleys - Paignton

Grid Reference: 887 623 —Landranger 202   Distance: 3.5 mile (2 hours)

This is another beautiful walk in Torbay, hidden in the valleys of Paignton. There is a small bit on the lead, but I don't mind because the rest of the walk is lovely. There are even glimpses of the sea on the way round.

1. Take the A380 from Torquay to Paignton, at the roundabout near Marldon turn left signposted Preston, this is Preston Down Road, follow the road and enjoy amazing views over the bay. Eventually, the road starts to descend steeply and has become Sandringham Gardens. Turn left into Hilton Drive, then take the third left into Old Paignton Road. At the bottom of the hill pull in and park on the left.
2. You need to put your lead on for a short while at the start. Walk back up Old Paignton Road. At the junction turn right back up Hilton Drive. Turn right at the top, and then cross into Upper Penns Road. At the end of the road you will see a gap in the hedge into some fields. Go through the gap. You can come off the lead now!
3. Turn right and follow the fields up the hill, staying on the higher paths when you can. I love to charge around through the grass here, the views of Torbay are amazing!
4. After a couple of fields the path will head into the woods (as long as you stay near the top of the fields). This path now runs along the valley through the woods, with the houses of Occombe Valley Road below you.
5. Follow the path until you reach another field. The way markers go left here down into the woods. You can either do this, or go straight across the field. Both paths rejoin later anyway.
6. Follow the path on up the valley. You will see a small stream down on your left. Eventually the lower path rejoins you via some steps.
7. You then reach a small wooden bridge that crosses the stream. Cross the bridge and carry on up the valley. Eventually you come to a gate.
8. Follow the track straight on past some new barn conversions. I would get your walker to put you on the lead here, as you will come out on Preston Down Road in a minute.

9. Once you hit the road turn right, and then cross the road and follow the lane that is signposted for Cockington, past Occombe Farm Shop. After about 100 metres you can take a footpath on the right that runs next to the lane.
10. Eventually the path turns right into Scadson Woods. Follow the path down through the woods, staying by the stream.
11. Eventually you will come out on a road. This is Old Paignton Road. Your car should be waiting.

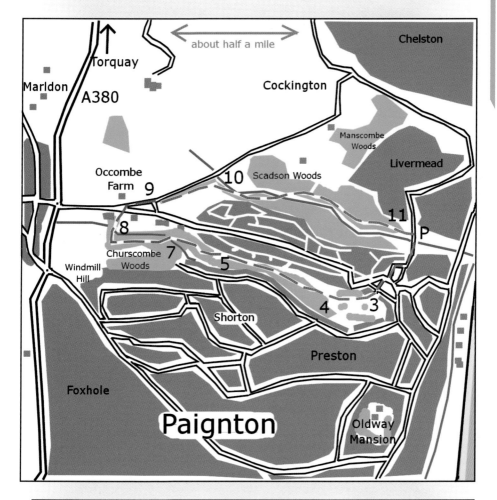

Playmates?	Y	Water to play in?	Y	Running space?	Y
Are there any hills?	Y	Any tricky stiles?	N	Car Parking?	Y
Are farm animals likely?	N	Poo Bins?	Y	Plenty of sticks?	Y

Walk 10 - Bovey River Nr. Lustleigh

Grid Reference: 790 801—Landranger 191   Distance: 4 miles (2 hours)

This is an amazing walk, surrounded by lush woodland and huge moorland hills you feel like you are in a lost world. Quite long and very uneven in places, but well worth the effort.

1. Take the A382 to Bovey Tracey. At the second roundabout outside Bovey (with Firestation on it) take a left towards Manaton. Follow the road towards Manaton. After about 2km take a right turn at Reddaford Water towards Lustleigh.
2. Drive along the lane until you see signs for Pullabrook Woods, Woodland Trust car park on the left. Pull in and park.
3. Now take the path that leads out of the car park into the woods.
4. This path heads up the River Bovey and slowly rises up away from the river. Follow the path through the woods until you reach another gate at the far end of the woods.
5. You are now entering the Dartmoor National Park. I would get your walkers to put you on a lead until you get back into the woods (its not far), just in case there are any livestock around. An obvious gravel track crosses your path turn right and follow this track down towards the next woods. Once you are back in the woods you can come off the lead.
6. Follow the track straight on until you meet an obvious track leading off right to the river. This takes you to Hisley Bridge. If you go this way you can follow the other side of the river back to the car park.
7. If you and your walkers are still bright eyed and waggy tailed you need to ignore the turn to Hisley Bridge and carry straight on up the left bank of the river, signposted for Manaton.
8. A bit further on you will see another footbridge on your right. Take this footbridge. When you get across, turn right and follow the track. You will then see English Nature signs welcoming you to Bovey Valley Woods.
9. You now follow this path for about a mile along the riverbank. If there has been heavy rain you will need to take a narrower path that runs along about 5 metres above the main path. The going is very uneven in places.
10. About two thirds of the way along you will see some amazing white water rapids and heaps of moss (which shows the air here is very clean!)
11. Eventually you will reach a very, very narrow footbridge that crosses the river. The bridge is made out of a cut tree which is flat on the top so you can walk across it. Cross the river here and head up the hill.

12. I would get your walker to put you on your lead here as there can sometimes be a few sheep in the woods.
13. At the next junction take the path on the right.
14. At the next junction take the path on the right again, that leads downhill back into English Nature woodland. Once you are in the woods it is safe to come off the lead again.
15. Follow the track through the woods until you reach a junction. Take the right hand path that leads down to the river and Hisley Bridge again.
16. Don't cross the bridge, but you can stop and play that good old game of Pooh sticks .Once you have finished your contest follow the path along the left bank of the river. Eventually you will reach a farmer's field. You need to cross the field and exit via the main gate.
17. Take a right turn down the lane back to the entrance to the car park.

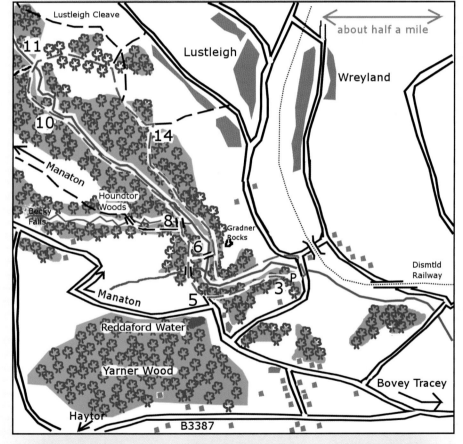

Playmates?	Y	Water to play in?	Y	Running space?	Y
Are there any hills?	Y	Any tricky stiles?	N	Car Parking?	Y
Are farm animals likely?	Y	Poo Bins?	N	Plenty of sticks?	Y

Walk 11 - Orley Common - Ipplepen

Grid Reference: 827 666—Landranger 202   Distance: 1 miles (45mins)

A fantastic short walk near Ipplepen. Once you have done the walk a few times you'll feel free to explore the common and make your walks as short or long as you want. My walkers enjoy sitting and admiring the stunning views across to Haytor, whilst I chase sticks.

1. Driving from Newton Abbot turn right off the A381 into Ipplepen at the first junction after Fermoy's Garden Centre. Follow the road through Ipplepen. It eventually loops right towards the church and becomes Orley Road. Follow the road out the other side of Ipplepen towards Torbryan. After about a mile you will see the entrance to Orley common on your left. Park in the car park on the right.
2. Make sure your walkers put you on a lead to cross the road. Cars can travel quickly along here. Once you have crossed the road into the entrance of Orley Common take the right hand track of the three in front of you. Follow the track into a tunnel of trees.
3. After a while the track splits into two, go left avoiding the steps. This path leads out into a small clearing.
4. Follow the path across the clearing into the next bit of woods. You come to a crossroads. Go straight ahead.
5. The path then splits again. This time take the right hand fork into the next clearing and follow the path across to the other side. At the far side of the clearing the path splits. Take the left hand path that leads back into the woods.
6. The path bares right and crosses another path, carry straight on down the hill in the woods. Further down the hill the path splits again. Take the slightly larger path to the left.
7. As you reach the bottom of the woods you join a large track coming up from the road below, join the track and turn left back up the hill, past an old quarry. We often see walkers hanging down on very long leads, their dogs must be very strong to pull them up the cliff face!

8. The path now follows the boundary between the woods and the fields on the right. Keep following the path as it runs up the hill near the wall. Ignore all left turns off the path. After about five minutes you will emerge at the end of the main common. Take the path that leads back into the woods on your right

9. This path goes through the woods until it bares sharp left at a five bar gate. My walkers often stop and look at the view here. Once you have enjoyed the view, carry on following the path as it follows the field wall. You will see a large divot in the woods on your left. Straight after this turn left into the woods and follow the path back onto the main common clearing.

10. Turn right and follow this big path back across the common. The views across to Haytor are stunning on a clear day. The bluebells are amazing in April.

11. Stay on this path and it will take you back to the entrance to Orley Common.

12. If your walkers now need a drink there is a great pub a little further down the road in Torbryan, or another great pub in Ipplepen.

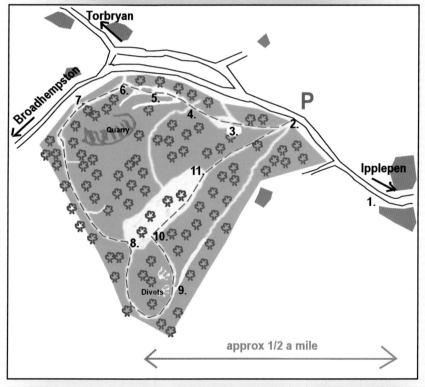

Playmates?	Y	Water to play in?	N	Running space?	Y
Are there any hills?	Y	Any tricky stiles?	N	Car Parking?	Y
Are farm animals likely?	N	Poo Bins?	Y	Plenty of sticks?	Y

Walk 12— The Exe Valley Canal

| Grid Reference: 900933—Landranger 192 | Distance: 6 miles (3hrs) |

This is a fabulous walk along the old Exeter Shipping canal. Now all you get is humans sat in plastic boats pushing themselves along with funny looking sticks. The flowers are beautiful in late May. My walker likes it because it has a pub at both ends!

1. Heading from Plymouth on the A38 or from Torquay on the A380 take the first turning into Exeter once you have come down Haldon Hill. Stay on this road until you get to the first roundabout, by the Devon Hotel. Take the second exit on the left into the industrial estate. Go straight across the next roundabout. Follow the road straight on. Go straight on at the traffic lights. At the next roundabout turn right. You then need to go straight ahead, the road bares right but you need to go straight on into the country lane in front of you. Over the bridge and then over the tight canal bridge. Now turn right and drive down the road that follows the canal. Eventually you reach the car parks for the Double Locks pub.
2. Park up and then cross the canal over the lock gates. Now carry on walking down the canal path.
3. Eventually you will see a large bridge up ahead. Get your walker to put you on the lead as the road is very, very busy. Cross the road using the traffic lights and carry on up the right hand side of the canal.
4. You will eventually walk under the M5 motorway bridge. Carry on up the canal path until you reach theTurf Lock pub at the other end. They let us doggies into the bar area, so make sure you take enough money to buy your walker a drink.
5. When your walkers are suitably refreshed, turn around and head back.

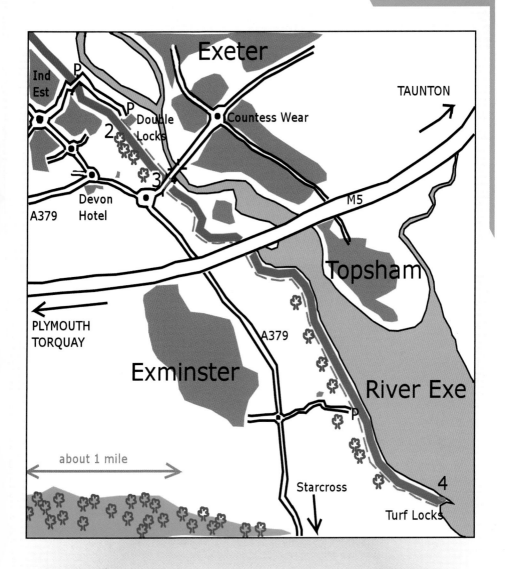

Playmates?	Y	Water to play in?	Y	Running space?	N
Are there any hills?	N	Any tricky stiles?	N	Car Parking?	Y
Are farm animals likely?	N	Poo Bins?	Y	Plenty of sticks?	N

Walk 13 - Mutter's Moor - Sidmouth

Grid Reference:108 873   Landranger 192   Distance: 3.5 miles (2 hrs)

This is a wonderful woodland walk with some far reaching views and rich carpets of bluebells in spring. There are more than enough paths to explore and space to roam about. It is very muddy in places after wet weather. The suggested walk is mainly level and at times undulating with one short sharp climb.

1. From junction 30 of the M5 at Exeter, take the A3052 towards Sidmouth. You will pass through Newton Poppleford, as you leave the village you will cross the River Otter. Take a right turn into a small country lane immediately after you cross the river. Then follow this road for about 3 miles as it follows the River Otter towards the sea, ignore all turn offs. Eventually you will reach a T-junction where you can turn right to Otterton or left to Sidmouth. You need to turn left to Sidmouth. Follow the road for about two miles, it will eventually start to climb a hill, then it will bend sharp right, after this bend you will find a car park a bit further on, on the left. Pull in and park up. I would get your walkers to put your lead on as it gets quite busy here.
2. Your walk starts in the bottom right hand corner of the car park (with your back to the road) where all the signs are.
3. Take the large gravel track that leads away from the car park into the woods and common.
4. After about 800m you will see a smaller track leading off to you left with a way-marker post pointing left. Follow this track. After a bit you will meet another larger gravel track. Turn left and stay on this track.
5. Follow the gravel track ignoring tracks leading off to the left. The track you are on will loop right around the outside of Mutter's Moor, so just enjoy the views and the gentle walk.
6. As the track loops around the top of the moor you will reach woodland again and the path will fork. Take the left path straight ahead.

7. After a while you will come to a junction of many paths, near a gateway into the next woods (Bulverton Hill). If your walkers are feeling waggy tailed you could go on up Bulverton Hill and follow the circular paths. Otherwise take the large gravel track on your right that descends to the golf course (watch out for balls!)
8. You will pass the 9th green, then you need to turn right and cross the course on the path provided, then follow the path up the steep hill opposite and back into the woods.
9. This path will eventually join the original gravel track leading from the car park. When you meet this large gravel track at a T-junction turn left and follow it back to the car.

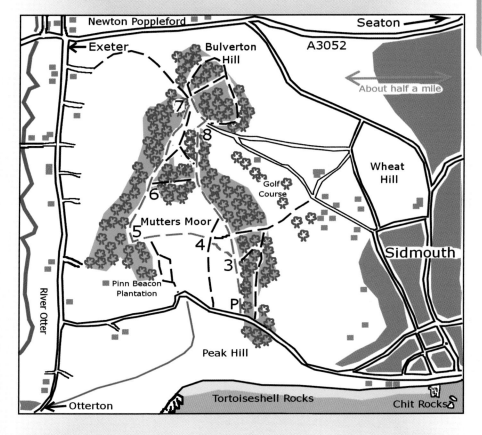

Playmates?	Y	Water to play in?	N	Running space?	Y
Are there any hills?	Y	Any tricky stiles?	N	Car Parking?	Y
Are farm animals likely?	N	Poo Bins?	Y	Plenty of sticks?	Y

Walk 14 - Lympstone Common

Grid Reference: 023 846 Landranger 192   Distance: 3.5 miles (2.5 hrs)

This is a really varied walk, with lovely woods, commons and stunning views. There are a few hills but no really steep ones. Allow lots of time for this walk.

1. From junction 30 on the M5 outside Exeter take the A376 towards Exmouth. Just after you pass the Lympstone Marine Base there is a left turn signposted towards Woodbury, take this turn. Then after about 50 metres take the first turning on the right up a small lane. Follow this lane straight on for about 2 miles ignoring any turn offs. Eventually you will reach a T-junction with a busier road. This is the B3180 to Budleigh Salterton. Turn right onto this road (take care as people drive quickly along this road). The road bends around to the left, on this bend there is a left turn uphill, take this turn. Then park up in the car park that is a bit further along on the left.
2. Now head into the woods at the back of the car park. Follow the path straight on. The path divides a bit, but rejoins itself again, but we recommend the left path.
3. You will eventually reach a single tree in a clearing. At the back of the clearing is a large drop. In the hollow you will sea lots of humps and bumps, and probably a few children doing jumps on their bikes. If you like chasing bikes, this is a good time to be on the lead.
4. The path leads off around the right hand side of the hollow. Follow the path off into the woods.
5. You will eventually come out onto an open common area. As you follow the track you will see Exeter off to your left. Keep following the track straight on as it heads downhill and narrows through some gorse bushes.
6. You will reach a fork in the track. Take the left path into the woods ahead of you. Follow this track until you meet a large bridleway running across your path in the woods. Turn right and follow the bridleway as it runs along through the woods. Ignore turnings off. You will eventually come out onto another common, with a lovely view to your right. Carry straight on.
7. As you reach the next bit of woodland, the path forks again. Take the left fork. You will come back up the right fork later on.

8. Follow this path right down through the woods to the road at the bottom. You will see Woodbury Common and large sand pits off to your right.
9. When you reach the road, cross into Upper Thorn Tree car park diagonally opposite.
10. The road in the car park sweeps around to the right. You need to take the path that goes off first left as you enter the car park. There is a low barrier across the path entrance to stop off-road vehicles using it.

11. Follow this path straight on across the common and through the woods. It gets narrow in places, but stick with the track until you reach the next road. You should come out opposite Wheat Hill car park.
12. Cross into the car park and follow the track leading out at the bottom of the car park on the left.
13. This track turns into a large gravel track that comes out on another common. Bare right when the track forks.
14. You will now head downhill into another wood, with fields on your right. After a while there will be a track leading back up through the woods on your right. Take this path.
15. Follow the path back up through the woods, ignore other paths, until you come to a t-junction. Turn right. Then at a fork take the left path. This takes you out onto a common again. Follow the path straight on uphill. After a while the path will narrow and become sandy underfoot. Ignore turns off to the left, staying on the uphill path, until your reach the road again.

16. Turn left along the road, and then right onto the first large track across the next common. There are two tracks take the very gravely track on the right. At a fork take the left track and follow this across the common to the next road ignoring turns that take you back downhill. There are fantastic views from here.
17. At the road there is a very narrow track straight opposite. Take this track back into the woods and follow it until it reaches a larger path.
18. Turn left on this path and you will come out at the fork where you went left near the start of the walk.
19. Follow this path back out onto the common and take the left path at the next fork that takes you back up the bridleway into the woods.
20. At the large bridleway signpost take a left and then immediately fork right. After a few metres take the small track on the right. Then follow the path baring left. This will bring you back out onto the first common with the view of Exeter on your right.
21. Go straight on into the woods ahead until you reach the biker's hollow. Then turn left towards the car park.

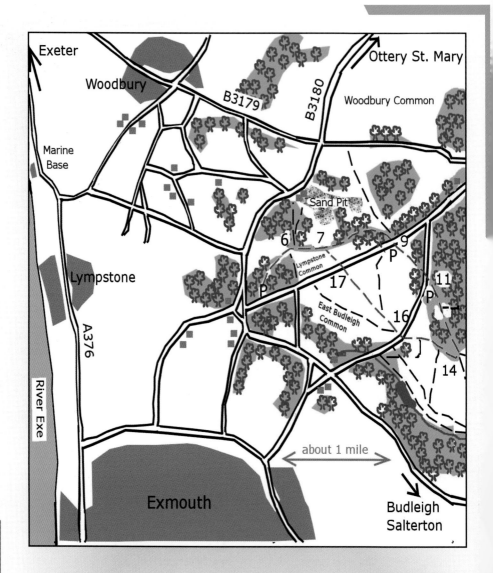

Playmates?	Y	Water to play in?	N	Running space?	Y
Are there any hills?	Y	Any tricky stiles?	N	Car Parking?	Y
Are farm animals likely?	N	Poo Bins?	Y	Plenty of sticks?	Y

Toby's Directory

DESPERATE DOG

Mobile Animal Care
Fully Insured
Pet Sitting / Dog Walking

Melanie Benham

Mobile:
07790 363664

National Petsitters
www.dogsit.com

Valley Pet Crematorium

Run for Pet owners, by Pet owners.

- **Personal Service/Individual Cremations**
- **Collection and delivery service**
- **Open door practice/ Domestic Pets Only**
- **Offer a final farewell in our St.Francis Room**

3 Gidley's Meadow, Christow,Exeter, EX6 7QB

Tel: 01647 253053
www.valleypetcrematorium.co.uk

TEACHERS PETS
All your pet care needs covered

Dog walking service—
Collection and return
Home visits to care for your pets
Dog boarding / Day creche in our home
Errands / House checks / Plant care

National Petsitters
www.dogsit.com

Contact Lorraine on:
Tel : 01752 563212
Mob: 07971 108012

A CLIPPING GOOD TIME

Sarah Louise Way
Old Umber Works
Chuley Road, Ashburton, TQ13 7DH
Dog Grooming
Tel:(01364) 652040
Or (01364) 631198

Toby's Directory